Counting in the Biomes

Counting in the Tundra

Fredrick L. McKissack, Jr. and Lisa Beringer McKissack

Enslow Elementary
an imprint of
Enslow Publishers, Inc.
40 Industrial Road
Box 398
Berkeley Heights, NJ 07922
USA

http://www.enslow.com

For Lisa's parents, Jan and Mark Beringer,
who took her to walk on tundra.

Enslow Elementary, an imprint of Enslow Publishers, Inc.

Enslow Elementary® is a registered trademark of Enslow Publishers, Inc.

Copyright © 2008 by Enslow Publishers, Inc.

Library of Congress Cataloging-in-Publication Data

McKissack, Fredrick, Jr.
    Counting in the tundra / Fredrick L. McKissack, Jr. and Lisa Beringer McKissack.
      p. cm. — (Counting in the biomes)
    Summary: "Children can count from one to ten as they read about the different animals found in the tundra"—Provided by publisher.
    Includes bibliographical references and index.
    ISBN-13: 978-0-7660-2989-7
    ISBN-10: 0-7660-2989-1
    1. Counting—Juvenile literature. 2. Tundra animals—Juvenile literature. 3. Biotic communities—Juvenile literature. I. McKissack, Lisa Beringer. II. Title.
    QA113.M39659 2008
    578.75'86—dc22

2007020294

Printed in the United States of America

10 9 8 7 6 5 4 3 2 1

To Our Readers: We have done our best to make sure all Internet Addresses in this book were active and appropriate when we went to press. However, the author and the publisher have no control over and assume no liability for the material available on those Internet sites or on other Web sites they may link to. Any comments or suggestions can be sent by e-mail to comments@enslow.com or to the address on the back cover.

Every effort has been made to locate all copyright holders of material used in this book. If any errors or omissions have occurred, corrections will be made in future editions of this book.

Illustration Credits: Corel Corporation, pp. 1, 5 (top), 27 (top); © Doug Allan/naturepl.com, pp. 5 (bottom), 6 (background), 7, 28–29 (background), 30–31 (background), 32 (background); James L. Amos/Photo Researchers, Inc., pp. 3 (background), 4 (background), 5 (background), 8–9 (background), 12–13 (background), 15 (inset), 16–17 (background), 24–25 (background), 26–27 (background), 28 (snow goose); Enslow Publishers, Inc., p. 4; © Nicola Gavin/Shutterstock, p. 11 (inset); © Barbara Gerlach/Visuals Unlimited, pp. 9 (left), 28 (snowshoe hare); Dan Guravich/Photo Researchers, Inc., pp. 3 (arctic ground squirrel), 20–21, 29 (arctic ground squirrel); © 2007 JupiterImages, pp. 3 (pasque flower, polar bear, snowy owl), 13, 17, 22 (inset), 27 (bottom), 28 (polar bear), 29 (pasque flower), 29 (snowy owl); © Steven J. Kazlowski/Alamy, pp. 22–23; Gerald C. Kelley/Photo Researchers, Inc., pp. 3 (snow goose), 14–15; George D. Lepp/Photo Researchers, Inc., pp. 2, 18–19, 29 (American pika); © Joe McDonald/Visuals Unlimited, pp. 3 (snowshoe hare), 9 (right); © 2007 Mark Newman/AlaskaStock.com, pp. 3 (tufted puffins), 25, 29 (tufted puffins); © Jerome Whittingham/Shutterstock, pp. 10–11, 26, 28 (arctic tern); Art Wolfe/Photo Researchers, Inc., pp. 6 (inset), 28 (arctic fox).

Cover Illustration: © 2007 JupiterImages.

Contents

Where in the world is the tundra?

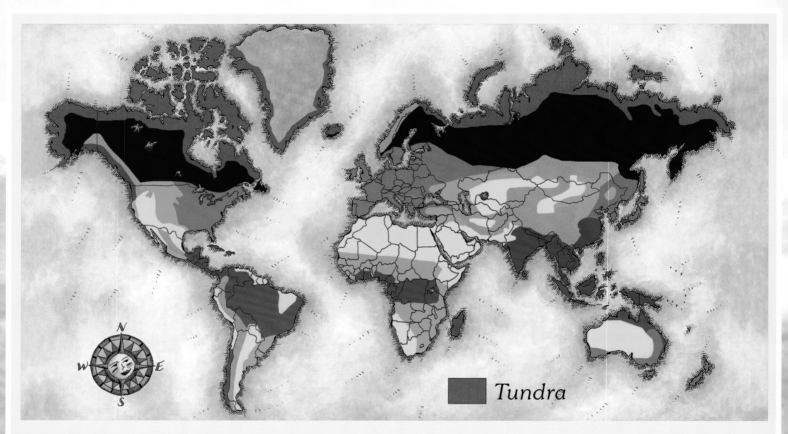

Tundra

What is a biome? A biome is an area of land or water with special plants and animals that need each other to live. There are many different kinds of biomes. Each biome has different kinds of weather.

In this book you will find out all about a place called the tundra.

tundra—A cold biome that has no trees. The winter is long and snowy. The summer is short and cool. Foxes, hares, polar bears, and other animals live there. There are two kinds of tundra: arctic and alpine.

alpine tundra—The kind of tundra found on the top of mountains. It is different from the arctic tundra. It does not hold water. Water flows down the mountain.

arctic tundra—The kind of tundra found at the North Pole. Its soil—called permafrost—stays frozen all year around.

How many **noses** does an arctic **fox** have?

One

The arctic fox is a good hunter. It has **one** nose to smell its prey. It walks very far to hunt for food.

A fox's fur changes color during the year. In winter, it is white. In summer, it is grayish brown. The fur helps the fox hide from other animals that may want to eat it.

How many **colors** does the **snowshoe hare** have?

Two

The snowshoe hare has **two** colors. It is brown in summer and white in winter. It uses the color change to hide. The hare also has big feet. These feet help the hare walk on snow.

Snowshoe hares live above ground. They hide under trees and bushes.

How many **colors** does the **arctic tern** have on its feathers?

Three

The arctic tern (TURN) is a bird. It has **three** colors on its feathers. The **three** colors are white, gray, and black.

Arctic terns live near the North Pole in the summer. They lay their eggs when the tundra is warm. When it starts to get cold, they fly all the way to the other end of Earth! By this time, it is summer at the South Pole. They fly further than any other bird on Earth—just to stay warm.

How many paws does a polar bear have?

Four

The oceans and rivers where polar bears live move quickly. This makes it hard to swim. The polar bear has **four** large paws for swimming. The front paws are like paddles on a boat. They make it easier for the polar bear to go through the fast moving water. The polar bear is the biggest bear in the world. Its **four** paws also help it run fast to catch food on land.

How many snow geese in a group fly south?

Five

Snow geese fly south for the winter. This group of **five** snow geese are flying south. In the summer, they fly back to the tundra.

A female snow goose has about **five** babies at one time. They nest in a small hole in the ground. The nest on the tundra is lined with plants and down feathers. This keeps the baby geese warm. Snow geese live with their babies until the first winter is over. After that, the young geese have to take care of themselves.

How many **petals** does a **pasque flower** have?

Six

Even though it is cold, flowers can grow in the tundra. The pasque (PASK) flower has about **six** petals. It grows along the sides of mountains. This helps it get lots of sunlight. The petals are white or purple.

Just like animals, the flower has to keep warm. It is small and grows very close to the ground. This helps it stay warm in the cold tundra wind.

How many **leaves** is this American **pika** eating?

Seven

The American pika (PIE-kuh) looks like a guinea pig. Pika live in alpine tundra. The rocks and trees help keep them safe and warm. It is also the best place to keep their food. They can put a lot of food in their mouths at once. This pika has **seven** leaves in its mouth! During the winter, they eat plants that they put away during the summer.

How many **front claws** does the arctic ground squirrel have?

Eight

The arctic ground squirrel is a small tundra animal. It has **eight** claws—four on each front paw. The squirrel uses its claws to hold food while it eats.

Arctic ground squirrels live in holes in the soft tundra ground. In the summer, they eat lots of food to store fat on their bodies. The cold winter is very hard on these little animals. They sleep underground in their nests all winter. Some of them sleep for seven months!

How many eggs in this snowy owl's nest?

Nine

This snowy owl's nest holds **nine** eggs. The eggs will hatch in about five weeks.

The snowy owl is a very big bird. Its wings are more than fifty inches from one end to the other. That is over four feet long. All snowy owls start with dark feathers. Only the males will become white over time.

How many tufted puffins do you see?

Ten

The tufted puffin is a bird of the tundra. They live in nests along arctic oceans and seas. Tufted puffins like to be with others. They hunt for fish in groups of about **ten**. The puffins will spend lots of time in the water getting fish for their families.

Tufted puffins stay in the tundra all year. They have special feathers that keep out water. This lets the birds swim for food, and stay dry and warm at the same time.

More Information on the Tundra

Tundra is a dry and cold biome. Most tundra is found in the far northern parts of the world. Some people think the South Pole is made of tundra. There is very little tundra there. Most of the South Pole is ice.

Tundra gets less than ten inches of water a year. In that way, it is like a cold desert. Much of its water comes from snow.

The word tundra means "barren land." The sun never goes down in the summer months. That is why tundra is also called "Land of the Midnight Sun."

There are two kinds of tundra: arctic tundra and alpine tundra. Arctic tundra is found close to the North Pole. It is soft like a sponge. It feels that way because the land traps and holds water. This ground is called peat. The ground below the tundra is as hard as a rock. This frozen ground is called permafrost.

Permafrost is ground that stays frozen all the time.

The second kind of tundra is alpine tundra. It is found high in the mountains. It is so high that trees do not grow very tall there. Alpine tundra does not hold as much water as arctic tundra. This is because the water runs down the side of the mountain.

In the winter, tundra gets very cold. Very few plants and animals are able to live in such a cold place.

Many animals leave the tundra during the winter months. Yet some have special skin, fur, or feathers that help keep them warm in the cold. The fur and feathers of some animals and birds change color. Some do it to hide from animals that want to eat them. Others change colors so the animals they hunt will not see them.

Count Again!

1		One
2		Two
3		Three
4		Four
5		Five

Count Again!

6		**Six**
7		**Seven**
8		**Eight**
9		**Nine**
10		**Ten**

Words to Know

arctic—Very cold places in the world near the North Pole.

barren—Land that has very few plants and animals.

North Pole—The northern most part of Earth.

peat—Dead plants that make soil.

permafrost—Ground that is always frozen.

prey—An animal that is eaten by another animal.

South Pole—The southern most part of Earth.

Learn More

Books

Green, Jen. *On the Tundra*. New York: Crabtree Publishing Company, 2002.

Stone, Lynn M. *Tundra*. Vero Beach, FL.: Rourke Pub., 2004.

Tagliaferro, Linda. *Explore the Tundra*. Mankato, Minn.: Capstone Press, 2007.

Internet Addresses

Tundra from the Missouri Botanical Garden
<http://www.mbgnet.net/sets/tundra/index.htm>

The Tundra Biome from the University of California Museum of Paleontology
<http://www.ucmp.berkeley.edu/exhibits/>
Click on "The World's Biomes." Click on "Tundra."

Index

A
alpine tundra, 5, 18, 26, 27
American pika, 18
arctic fox, 6
arctic ground squirrel, 20
arctic tern, 10
arctic tundra, 5, 26

B
biome, 4, 26

C
changing colors, 6, 8, 27
claws, 20
cold, 10, 16, 20, 26, 27

E
eggs, 10, 22

F
feathers, 10, 14, 22, 24, 27
fur, 6, 27

L
leaves, 18

M
mountains, 5, 27

N
North Pole, 5, 26

P
pasque flower, 16
paws, 12, 20
peat, 26

permafrost, 5, 26, 27
petals, 16
polar bear, 12

S
sleep, 20
snow goose, 14
snowshoe hare, 8
snowy owl, 22
South Pole, 26
swimming, 12, 24

T
tufted puffin, 24
tundra, 4, 5, 14, 16, 20, 24, 26, 27

Northport-East Northport Public Library

To view your patron record from a computer, click on
the Library's homepage: **www.nenpl.org**

You may:
- request an item be placed on hold
- renew an item that is overdue
- view titles and due dates checked out on your card
- view your own outstanding fines

**185 Larkfield Road
East Northport, NY 11731
631-261-2313**